Looking Back

AUTHOR'S NOTE

A majority of the questions and answers in this book were gathered first hand from senior citizens as they remember days long ago or as they recall their parents telling about *their* days. Consequently, you may well remember differently than they, and your answers may be slightly different. Though much research has gone into making this book as accurate as possible, the author realizes that a book based on personal interviews always leaves room for error. If you the reader have a different answer for the questions in this book, it is entirely possible yours may be more correct than those remembered by others. Yet the real purpose of this book is simply to provide lively reminiscing among senior citizens as well as informing the younger generations of a life in an era they will never know. I hope it will bring you personally, and if you are an activity leader, your group, many happy hours of reminiscing. God bless you all.

Looking Back

By
Marge Knoth

Valley Press
Lafayette, Indiana

Copyright © 1989 by Marge Knoth

ALL RIGHTS RESERVED

No part of this book may be reproduced in any form or by any electronic means without written permission from the author with the exception being that a reviewer may quote a brief passage for a review.

Library of Congress Card Catalog Number: 89-051218
ISBN Number: 0-927935-01-5

First Printing: July, 1989
Second Printing: February, 1990
Third Printing: November, 1990
Fourth Printing: March, 1991
Fifth Printing: May, 1991
Sixth Printing: October, 1993
Seventh Printing: March, 1996

WAYS TO USE *LOOKING BACK*

Looking Back is a small book, yet it is a treasury of information that will bring many happy hours of reminiscing. It may be used for individual reading enjoyment, for conversation openers with the elderly, for party entertainment, or for leading a lively reminiscent group. Following are a few variations of its use with groups.

* A group of people may be divided into two teams. A question from *Looking Back* is asked a person on team one. If he gets the question right, his team scores one point. A team two member then gets a chance to answer the next question. If team one *misses* their question, team two has the opportunity for one of their people to answer it. If they do so correctly, they receive two points for being able to answer a missed question. If neither team can answer it, go on to the next question. This game may be continued as long as desired. You'll find it hard to limit the time because everyone will want to reminisce.

* In a small or large group setting a senior citizen may be given any question in *Looking Back* and be asked to talk about the subject as he remembers it for two minutes. If he succeeds he (or his team if you have formed teams) receives one point. If a person talks longer than three minutes he loses his point. When two minutes are completed, a warning card should be held up to let the player know he has only one minute to wind up his conversation. The person or team with the most points wins. Be sure each player gets equal opportunities to answer.

* Arrange players in a circle. Ask the question. Everyone who knows the answer raises his hand. No one may speak out until recognized by the leader. The first hand to be raised is allowed to answer. If he answers correctly he receives a point. If he misses, the second person who raised his hand is given a chance to answer. This may require the leader to write down the first three who raise their hands. If by the third player the question remains unanswered, go on to the next question.

* The *Looking Back* answer may be acted out in charades form with those in attendance guessing what the old days subject is.

* *Looking Back* may be used simply as a discussion starter to lead a reminiscent group.

DEDICATION

Looking Back is dedicated to my four children--Lisa, Nick, April and Toni who through their growing up years spent countless hours at the nursing home assisting with activities as well as showing remarkable patience with their mother who daily delighted in retelling residents' stories about happenings in an era long before their time.

TABLE OF CONTENTS

Section One

1) Movies, Length
2) Movies, Time
3) Movies, Close-up
4) Blacking Kitchen Stove
5) Baking With Feather Bed
6) Halley's Comet
7) Parching Corn
8) Potato Wine
9) 52/20 Club
10) Sewing Patterns
11) Pyramid Clubs
12) Crossword Puzzles
13) Paper Dolls
14) Church Pew Rental
15) Overland Car
16) Heating Curling Irons
17) Cleaning Coal Oil Lamps
18) Election Reports
19) W.W. 1 Soldier's Pay
20) Soldiers March on Washington
21) Jack Benny's Maxwell
22) Repairing Runs in Hosiery
23) Paper Beads
24) National Relief Organization
25) Buckeye Salve

Section Two

26) Cereal Box Puppets
27) Hoover House
28) Hoover Flag

29) Hoover Blanket
30) Summer Kitchen
31) Spoon Holders
32) Food Storage
33) Flag Pole Sitting
34) What Five Cents Will Buy
35) Cost of Cigarettes
36) Treating Moths
37) Mice Remedies
38) First Ticketed Speeder
39) Model T Battery Aid
40) Gold Star in Window
41) Model B Car
42) Trash Disposal
43) Base Burner
44) Hospital Fear
45) Round Barns
46) Storm Wagon or Klondike
47) The Slip of a Lip Can Sink a Ship
48) Hair Setting Lotion
49) First Income Tax
50) Liquor in Wooden Barrels

Section Three

51) Celluloid Collars
52) Courthouse Square
53) Carpet Beaters
54) Chalk Boards
55) Community Dipper
56) Digging Mussels and Clams
57) Circuit Riders
58) Troop Trains
59) Maternity Care
60) Country Store
61) Wooden Barrels
62) Storing Produce

63) Movie Price
64) Ice Man
65) Making Turpentine
66) Carbide Gas
67) Laundry Soap
68) Air in Coleman Lamps
69) Lamplighter
70) Dollar Size
71) Pierced Ears
72) Salt Packaging
73) Corn Husking Bees
74) Corn Husking Bees (2)
75) Pocket Knife

Section Four

76) Making Scouring Powder
77) Making Sausage
78) Grinding Walnuts
79) Poultice
80) Hominy
81) Dating
82) Barney Google
83) Head Lice
84) Rolling Snow
85) Boot Jacks
86) Weather in 1937
87) WPA
88) WPA Jobs
89) CCC
90) Amelia Earhart's Drink
91) Dan Patch
92) Wash Day
93) Wash Beans
94) Lindbergh Baby Kidnapping
95) Who Kidnapped Baby
96) Al Capone

97) Brick Foot Warmers
98) Shoe Shine Boy
99) April Fool's Candy
100) School Age

Section Five

101) Yard Measure
102) Inch Measure
103) Horse's Height Measure
104) Car License Plates
105) Cornstarch for Powder
106) Cheek Coloring
107) The Charleston
108) Knute Rockney
109) Babe Ruth
110) Gertrude Eberle
111) Children's Games
112) Dunce Cap
113) Will Rogers
114) Death Practices
115) Butchering
116) Liver Pudding
117) Root Cellar
118) Porcelain Dishes
119) School Reader
120) Rudolph Valentino
121) Rudy Vallee
122) Stock Market Crash
123) Clara Bow
124) Raccoon Coat
125) Near Beer

Section Six

126) Consumption
127) Infantile Paralysis
128) Franklin Roosevelt
129) Diphtheria
130) Quarantine
131) Pest House
132) Alice Huyler Ramsey
133) Oil of Citronella
134) Cockroach Hotels
135) Flypaper
136) Smoke For Earache
137) Goose Grease
138) Complexion Treatments
139) Steam Calliope
140) Elephants Working
141) Frank Sinatra
142) Stockings In A Bottle
143) Zoot Suit
144) Making Soap
145) Titanic
146) S.O.S.
147) Lane Bryant
148) Pregnancy
149) Watkins and Raleigh Man
150) Marks Brothers

Section Seven

151) Speakeasy
152) Dionne Quintuplets
153) Haircuts of 1920's
154) Zeppelin
155) Fred Astaire and Ginger Rogers
156) Gone With the Wind

157) Clark Gable
158) Miniature Golf Craze
159) Hairpins for Model T Fixing
160) Leaky Radiator
161) Overheated Radiator
162) First Highway
163) Speed Limit
164) Before Windshield Wipers
165) Barbershop Pole
166) Halloween Toy
167) Chatauqua
168) Chivaree
169) Women Smoking
170) Testing Oven Temperature
171) Wallpaper Cleaner
172) Furniture Polish
173) Thawing the Old Pump
174) Asafetida Bag
175) Cream on Milk

Section Eight

176) Circus Evolution
177) Circus Sayings
178) Hobo
179) WPA Founder
180) Model T Tires
181) Electric Car
182) First Race
183) Race Speed
184) First 500
185) Depression Tactics
186) Protection Tax
187) Horses on Ice
188) Sleds From Lard Can Lids
189) Boot on Tire
190) Truman's Girls

191) Lemonade Jingle
192) Victory Bread
193) Radio Programs
194) Wiley Post
195) Revenue Officers
196) License Plates Life Span
197) Little Orphan Annie
198) Lengthening Life of Sheet
199) Underwear From Feed Sacks
200) Gypsies

EXTRAS FOR YOU

- Do You Remember?
  (100 more discussion starters)   63

- Home Cooking   75

- Child's Play   77

- The Movie Scene (1930)   79

- Other Books by the Author   82

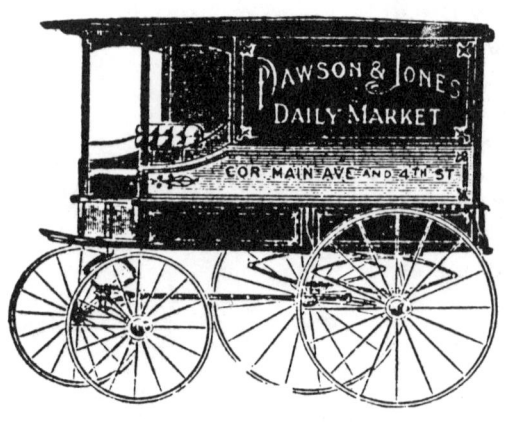

Section One

1) How long did the very early movies last?

   About ten minutes.

2) Why were the movies only ten minutes long?

   Because movie makers felt they couldn't hold their audience's attention any longer than that.

3) Why did the early movies never show close-ups of people?

Because they thought the audience would feel cheated seeing only half a person.

4) Why was the old kitchen stove blackened regularly?

To prevent it from rusting.

5) How were feather beds used for baking long ago?

As soon as one got up in the morning when the bed was still warm, a bowl of bread dough would be placed between two feather mattresses to rise.

6) Long ago, how did you look at Halley's Comet?

Through glass that had been smoked.

7) How did you make a drink from corn during hard times?

You parched the corn in a skillet and made a drink resembling coffee.

8) What drink did you make from potato peels to keep from wasting them?

Wine.

9) What was the 52/20 Club?

> Discharged service men after World War II received $20 a week for 52 weeks.

10) What did you use for sewing patterns long ago?

> You ripped up old clothes and used them for patterns.

11) What were the nation-wide Pyramid clubs during the 1940's?

> They were similar to chain letters where you were to send in a little money and supposedly get back $2,048.

12) When did the first book of crossword puzzles come out?

> In 1924.

13) Where did young girls long ago get paper dolls?

> They cut them from models in the Sears Catalog and also *McCall's* magazine featured a paper doll in each issue called "Betsy McCall."

14) Besides the regular Sunday collection at church, why else was money paid to the church each week? Sometimes this fee was paid in a yearly lump sum.

You paid for your seat.

15) What old-time car had the gear shift on the outside?

    The Overland.

16) How did ladies heat their curling irons before electricity?

    They put them down in the lamp flue till they were hot.

17) After cleaning them, why did homemakers cover glass coal oil lamps during the day with paper bags?

    To keep the flies off them.

18) How did one receive election news or news of the World Series before there was radio in homes?

    They went to the town newspaper office and stood outside where editors would hold up signs to the crowd gathered outside.

19) How much was a soldier's pay during World War I?

    $30.00 a month with $1.00 extra for overseas pay.

20) After World War I, soldiers marched on Washington. Why?

To collect the extra dollar a month they were supposed to receive for overseas pay.

21) Jack Benny on his radio show often talked about his car. What kind was it?

Maxwell.

22) Long ago, what did women do when they got a run in their hose?

They took them to a hosiery store for repair or they sewed them up themselves.

23) Remember making paper beads for jewelry. How did you do it?

You cut colorful or black and white magazine pages into triangle strips and rolled them around a big hat pin. You then dipped them in glue and let them dry. They were next varnished. When dry again, the hat pin would be removed and they were strung with a needle and thread.

24) In Franklin D. Roosevelt's presidency, what was one thing the NRA (National Relief Association) did?

It cut the work week to five days and hoped to put more people to work by so doing.

25) What medicine was made by frying buckeyes in grease?

A salve for wounds.

Section Two

26) In the old days, what treats did kids sometimes find on the outside of cereal boxes?

   Clowns and puppets that could be cut out and assembled.

27) What was the *Hoover House?*

   An outdoor toilet.

28) What were Hoover flags?

> They were individuals running around with their pants pockets turned inside out signifying that the Hoover administration was responsible for the hard times.

29) What were Hoover blankets?

> Newspapers.

30) What was the summer kitchen?

> A separate kitchen located in an area such as an outside enclosed porch where cooking and canning were done in hot weather in order to keep the heat out of the main house.

31) What were spoon holders and where did they usually set?

> They resembled a fancy vase, usually glass, and they held spoons. Generally they were kept on the middle of the table.

32) How were upstairs rafters used for storing food long ago?

> Meat, in winter, was often hung from them because it was colder there. Spices were also hung there to dry.

33) How, besides displaying flags, were flag poles used long ago?

For flagpole sitting.

34) Name some things five-cents used to buy.

A box of Crackerjacks, a big pickle, a Coke, several pencils, piece of pie, two cigars, a tube of BB shots or a red and green top to spin.

35) Remember when cigarettes sold separately. How much did they cost?

One cent each.

36) What common household food was used to get rid of moths?

Salt.

37) What was one thing, long ago, used to fight mice?

Pumpkin seeds.

38) Who was the first recorded ticketed speeder?

A New York cabbie was ticketed for going twelve miles an hour.

39) Can you remember when a mixture of kerosene and gasoline was poured into the carburetor of your old Model T? Why was it done?

If it wasn't done, your battery might run down trying to get enough gas to make it run.

40) During the War, why was a gold star hung in the window of a soldier's home address?

It meant *that* mother had lost her son in the war.

41) What model (letter) car was manufactured between 1904 and 1905 and was replaced by the Model K?

Model B.

42) What were some ways garbage was disposed of before trash pick-up?

It was burned or sometimes dumped in the river. Farmers fed it to hogs.

43) What had to be done with the base burner every spring and every fall?

It was taken down in the spring and put up in the fall.

44) Why, long ago, were people afraid to go to the hospital?

People felt hospitals were only a place to die.

45) Why were some round barns built?

To eliminate corners where it was sometimes difficult to store hay.

46) What was the storm wagon or the Klondike?

A glass enclosed buggy.

47) What was a famous saying about a ship during World War II?

"The slip of a lip can sink a ship."

48) What hair setting lotion was made from a common food?

Sugar water.

49) When was the first income tax started?

1913.

50) What kind of containers did big quantities of liquor use to come in?

Wooden barrels.

Section Three

51) What were the stiff collars men used to wear made of?

    Celluloid.

52) When folks used to come to town on Saturday night, where did they gather to visit with their friends?

    Around the courthouse square.

53) Before vacuum cleaners, how did the homemaker get the dirt out of her rugs?

She hung the rugs over the line and beat them with a carpet beater.

54) How were the very first chalk boards hung in the classrooms?

They were hung from the ceiling by rope.

55) If you wanted a drink of water at school long ago, where did you get it and from what did you drink?

There was a water bucket in the back of the room with a community dipper in it for everyone.

56) Why did many folks dig mussels and clams?

They gathered the shells and sold them to button factories to make buttons.

57) What were traveling preachers on horseback called?

Circuit riders.

58) Remember troop trains coming through towns as the soldiers were going off to war. What did the homefolk put in the soldiers' hands as they reached out the windows?

Home-baked cookies and other goodies.

59) Can you remember how much it cost for nine months of maternity care and delivery during the 1920's?

$25.00 and sometimes less.

60) Remember shopping at the old country store? In what kind of containers would you find pickles, peanut butter and crackers?

Big wooden barrels.

61) You used to buy coffee beans at the store. How and when did you grind them?

When you got home before they were to be used. You ground them in a little wooden box with a crank handle on the top.

62) How were vegetables like carrots and potatoes, and fruits like apples kept outside during the winter without freezing?

A hole was dug in the ground and they were put there and then covered with straw and then with dirt. They were dug up as needed.

63) How much did it cost to go to a movie in the 1920's?

Five cents mostly, sometimes ten, but the balcony seats were usually less expensive.

64) When you were expecting the ice man, what did the little signs you hung in your kitchen window say?

25#, 50#, or whatever weight you wanted.

65) What did you use to make turpentine?

The sap that oozed out of pine trees.

66) What kind of gas was used to light miners caps, car head lights, to make fireworks, and to scare fish when fishing?

Carbide.

67) Name an old brand of laundry soap that came in a bar.

Star City and P & G are two.

68) How did one get air into gas or Coleman lamps?

They used something that looked like a bicycle pump.

69) How did the oil street lights get lit?

A lamplighter appeared each evening with his little stool. He climbed up and lit the street light. Each morning he came back to put the flame out.

70) The dollar bill wasn't always the size it is now. How did it differ?

It was longer and wider, about a half inch each way.

71) Long ago folks had their ears pierced for reasons other than beauty. Do you remember why?

They thought it would help their eyes.

72) How was salt packaged long ago and how much did it cost?

It came in a cloth bag and sold for a dime.

73) Remember corn husking bees of long ago? What were the young men looking for?

A red ear of corn.

74) In the old-time corn-husking bees, what happened to the young man who found the red ear?

He got to kiss his favorite girl.

75) Long ago you could buy top quality leather shoes for men from Montgomery Wards's for $3.98. If you paid an extra dollar, you could get them with a special little holder built into the side of a shoe with something inside it. What was in the holder?

A nice shiny knife.

Section Four

76) What in the old days was used to make scouring powder?

Sifted ashes.

77) When making sausage, some people used to jack up the back wheel of the old Model T to get the job done. Why?

The hand grinder would be attached to the spokes to grind the meat into sausage.

78) How did you use that old car for walnuts?

You ran over them to crack the hulls off and some even took the tire off, jacked up the wheel and poured walnuts in the rim of the wheel to hull them.

79) Turpentine and bacon fat were used when someone had an infection. Why?

They were used to pull out an infection.

80) What did you pour over white corn on the cob to make hominy?

Lye water.

81) Was it proper for a young lady long ago to date more than one fellow at a time?

No. She was considered loose if she did.

82) What was Barney Google famous for?

His goo-goo-googly eyes.

83) What was used in the old days to treat head lice?

Carbolic acid and coal oil were applied with a feather applicator.

84) There used to be another way to take care of snow rather than shoveling it. What was it?

You rolled the snow.

85) What instrument did men use to remove their boots?

Boot jacks.

86) What was history's hottest summer and coldest winter?

1937.

87) With 13 million workers laid off during the Great Depression, what government program helped put men and women to work?

WPA

88) What were some of the jobs that the WPA workers did?

Built sidewalks, outdoor toilets, roads; painted and danced.

89) What government program during the 30's put young men ages 17 to 24 to work planting trees, keeping up parks and building dams?

The CCC or Civilian Conservation Corp.

90) What was Amelia Earhart's favorite drink?

Buttermilk.

91) Who was the famous race horse who never lost a race during his prime career between 1900 and 1909?

Dan Patch

92) What day of the week long ago was always considered wash day?

Monday.

93) What food was most often served on wash day?

Beans. They called them "wash beans."

94) Who was the baby who was kidnapped from his famous father's home in 1932? The whole world mourned with the parents when he was reported dead.

The son of the famous flier Charles A. Lindbergh.

95) Who was the man found guilty of kidnapping the Lindbergh baby and sent to the electric chair even though his wife, in her old age, continued to declare his innocence?

Bruno Richard Hauptmann

96) Who was the famous gangster of the 30's whose nickname was "Scarface?"

Al "Scarface" Capone

97) In the old buggy, in wintertime, how were feet kept warm?

Bricks were heated at home before the trip and were wrapped up and feet were placed on them during the trip.

98) What job might a young boy hold at a barbershop?

A shoe shine boy.

99) Remember April Fool's candy long ago? What was it?

Cotton-stuffed chocolate drops, caramel-covered wood, pepper-filled bon bons.

100) What was an old-time way of telling if a boy was old enough to go to school?

He was old enough if he could reach over his head and touch his other ear with his hand.

Section Five

101) How was a yard measured without a yard stick?

It was measured from the tip of one's nose to the end of his outstretched hand.

102) How was an inch measured?

From the tip of one's thumb to his first thumb joint.

103) How was a horse's height measured?

It was measured in hands, so many hands high.

104) What were the first car license plates like?

They were homemade. Some were wood with numbers carved in them. Others were scrap metal with numbers riveted in them.

105) When women first started to paint their faces around the early 1900's, what kitchen product did they use for powder?

Flour or cornstarch.

106) What form of food packaging did they use to color their cheeks?

The red mesh bags potatoes and onions came in. They wet them and rubbed them on their cheeks. Also they used tissue paper the same way.

107) What famous dance came out in the 1920's?

The Charleston. Also the Black Bottom.

108) Who was the famous football coach of Notre Dame?

Knute Rockney.

109) Who was the baseball king who hit 60 home runs in 1927?

Babe Ruth.

110) Who was the first woman to swim the English Channel in the 1920's?

Gertrude Eberle. She beat the men's record by 2 1/2 hours.

111) What were *Annie Annie Over, Shinney on Your Own Side* and *Duck on Davey?*

They were games played by children.

112) What was a *dunce cap?*

They were tall hats placed on the head of a student who misbehaved in school. It was shameful to wear one.

113) What famous personality was called the *Restless Roper?* He was also a comedian, writer and a spokesman.

Will Rogers

114) When were mirrors covered and clocks stopped?

When there was a death in a home.

115) When was butchering day usually held?

Around Thanksgiving, after a good frost.

116) What was liver pudding?

On butchering day, liver pudding was made by grinding pork liver, jowls, heart and ears. Seasonings were added and it was boiled in a cloth bag and then packed in cleaned intestines. It would then be hung on a hickory post in the smoke house.

117) What was a root cellar?

It was a storage place for vegetables and fruit. Sometimes it was a cave-like place in the ground with a door where you walked down steps into it.

118) From what material were your dishes made?

Often it was porcelain.

119) During your early school days, what was the common reader used?

The McGuffey reader.

120) Who was the famous male movie star of silent films who died at a young age and women wept hysterically. A famous reindeer has the same name as the actor's first name?

Rudolph Valentino.

121) Who was the famous crooning singer of the 1920's?

Rudy Vallee.

122) What year did the famous stock market crash take place?

1929.

123) Who was the famous red headed lady movie star of long ago who scooted around Hollywood in her red convertible with seven red chow dogs? She was called the "it" girl. Her name is the same as something girls wear in their hair.

Clara Bow.

124) What kind of long fur coat was worn by men and women alike during the 1920's.

The racoon coat.

125) What was *near beer?*

During prohibition, it was a drink like beer but had 99% of the alcohol removed.

Section Six

126) What was another name for T.B. in the old days?

Consumption.

127) What was polio called as late as the 1940's?

Infantile paralysis.

128) What U.S. president suffered from infantile paralysis?

Franklin D. Roosevelt.

129) What was the main symptom of diphtheria?

A sore throat.

130) When one had small pox or other contagious diseases, a sign would be posted on their front door. What did it say?

Quarantined.

131) Sometimes there was a special building where people with contagious diseases were kept till they were well. What was it called?

The pest house.

132) Who was the first woman to drive a car across America? The year was 1909.

Alice Huyler Ramsey.

133) What, long ago, was rubbed on your skin to keep mosquitos away?

Oil of citronella.

134) What were cockroach houses? Some called them cockroach hotels.

   They were little house-like structures that were placed in cupboards to kill cockroaches.

135) What was the sticky stuff you hung from the ceiling to catch flies?

   Flypaper.

136) How was smoke used to help an earache?

   It was blown in the ear.

137) Why was goose grease rubbed on the palm of the hands, the soles of the feet and the chest?

   To fight a cold.

138) What fruit used to be rubbed on the face to treat complexion problems?

   Watermelon. Sometimes lemon.

139) As the circus parade would pull into town, the last wagon one would see would be the steam calliope. How many whistles did it give?

   Thirty-two.

140) Who did the heavy work of setting up and dismantling the circus tents?

The elephants.

141) Who was the 1940's teenage singer who crooned his melodies. Teenagers loved him but parents often hated him.

Frank Sinatra.

142) What was *stockings in a bottle?*

It was liquid leg make-up used during the war when hose were hard to get.

143) What was the zoot suit?

It was a suit worn by men with an oversize jacket. A bow tie was worn and a long chain hung almost to the floor.

144) When making soap, what were the two main ingredients?

Grease and lye.

145) What 1912 ship was said to be unsinkable?

The Titanic.

146) Who sent the first S.O.S. in history?

> The Titanic. S.O.S. was just a new international code of distress agreed upon at a recent convention. When the Titanic couldn't summon help when sinking, they tried the S.O.S.

147) How did Lane Bryant begin her dress selling career?

> She designed a tea gown for pregnant women--the first real maternity wear ever made. It became so popular that she designed a whole line of maternity wear. Her real name was Lena Bryant. She began in 1910.

148) Long ago what words were used to describe being pregnant?

> A lady in waiting, lying in, being in a family way or being in a delicate condition.

149) What were some main products the Watkins and the Raleigh man carried as they delivered door-to-door?

> Vanilla, spices, food coloring, liniments, kidney pills, salve, shoe polish, etc.

150) What were the Marks brothers names?

> Groucho, Chico, Harpo, and Zeppo.

Section Seven

151) What was the speakeasy?

It was an establishment like a bar popular during prohibition where alcoholic drinks were sold illegally.

152) Who were the very famous quintuplets born in a farm house in 1934 in Ontario, Canada?

The Dionne quintuplets.

153) What were two of the famous bob hair cuts during the 1920's?

The Egyptian bob and the shingle *bob.*

154) What was the Zeppelin?

It was a type of rigid airship first designed around 1900. Some exploded killing many passengers.

155) Who was the famous dance team of the 1930's who also made movies?

Fred Astaire and Ginger Rogers.

156) What 1930's movie star stole audiences' hearts with her performance in *Gone With the Wind?*

Vivian Leigh.

157) Who was her male counter star?

Clark Gable.

158) What wild sports craze swept America during the summer of 1930 causing Americans to spend a million dollars a day on the game?

Miniature golf.

159) What simple item used by women could often fix a Model T engine?

A hairpin.

160) What household food was sometimes used to plug a leaky radiator?

Oatmeal.

161) How would an overheated radiator be checked?

By spitting on it.

162) When did the first coast-to-coast highway come into use?

1927.

163) In 1935 what was the maximum speed on the highways?

35 mph.

164) Before windshield wipers on cars, what trick was sometimes used to keep windows clean when it rained?

Before it rained, a raw onion that had been cut in half was rubbed on the windshield.

165) What item hung outside a barbershop that let you know a barbershop was located there?

   A red, white and blue pole.

166) What was a homemade toy called *rattlebones?*

   It was made with a wooden spool and its main feature was to make noise on someone's window on Halloween.

167) What was the chatauqua?

   In the days before automobiles were common and before movie houses were popular, it was a traveling show that came to a town and featured performances that ran daily for several days. Often they were of a spiritual nature.

168) What happened at a chivaree?

   A newly wed couple, when they were supposedly asleep, would be initiated by friends and relatives who stood outside the couple's home and rang bells and banged pots and pans together to make noise. The visitors would then be invited inside for refreshments.

169) Long, long ago, women usually didn't smoke, but when they became of grandmotherly age, they often did? Why?

54

It was said to help stomach ailments.

170) Using the old iron cook stove without temperature control, how did a homemaker test to see if the temperature was right to bake her cake?

She would put her hand in the oven, and she knew by the feel if it was too hot or too cold.

171) What household food was cooked and used to make wallpaper cleaner?

Cornmeal. It was cooked and then worked with the hands till elastic-like and then was rubbed on the walls almost like an eraser.

172) How was furniture polish made long ago?

Linseed oil and kerosene were mixed together.

173) When the old pump froze up in winter, what did you do?

You poured boiling water on it.

174) To ward off sickness mothers often made their children wear a smelly bag around their necks. What was it called?

Asafetida bag.

175) When the milkman brought milk to your door in bottles, what had to be scooped off the top of the milk before it was ready to pour?

Cream.

Section Eight

176) Where did the circus actually evolve from?

The Romans who used to pit man against beast or beast against beast. It came to America in the 19th century.

177) Where did the sayings *Hold your horses, Get the show on the road, and Come rain or shine* come from?

They originated with the circus.

178) If once you fed a hobo, what was sure to happen to your house?

Your house would be a mark, and you'd be sure to have more hobos stop by for a hand-out.

179) What president was responsible for starting the WPA?

Franklin Roosevelt.

180) What size tires did the Model T use?

30 by 3 1/2.

181) What type of car was popular between 1900 and 1915 and was considered a ladies car?

The electric car.

182) Where and when was the first recorded automobile race?

It was held in 1895 and the race was from Chicago to Evanston.

183) What was the average speed of that first race?

5 mph.

184) What year was the first 500 mile race in Indianapolis, Indiana held?

1911.

185) During the Great Depression, farmers received less for their crops and animals than it took to produce them. In an effort to raise prices, what did they do?

They dumped their milk and slaughtered their animals.

186) Al Capone devised a way to keep small businesses from being robbed by gangsters. He placed a tax on them. It was really blackmail, but what did Al Capone call it?

A protection tax.

187) Long ago, how were horses' feet protected during the winter to keep them from slipping on the ice?

Gunny sacks were tied to their feet.

188) Many folks long ago couldn't afford sleds for their kids. What common item used in food packaging did they use to slide down hills on?

Lard can lids.

189) What did it mean to put a boot on a tire?

> You saved pieces from old tires and attached these with glue to the tire you were repairing.

190) President Truman had two favorite girls. He had a special name for each. His wife was his sweetheart. Who was his other special girl and what did he call her?

> It was his mother and he called her his *best girl.*

191) There used to be a childhood game called *Lemonade.* What was the jingle that went with it?

> "Here we come. Where from? New Orleans. What's your trade? Lemonade. Show us some." (Then you acted out your trade.)

192) What was *victory bread?*

> It was rough-grained bread eaten rather than soft bread to help the war effort.

193) What were *Ma Perkins, Inner Sanctum, and Amos and Andy?*

> They were radio programs.

194) Who was the one-eyed pilot of the 1930's who was twice honored at the White House by President Truman. He was a friend of Will Rogers.

Wiley Post.

195) Bootleggers were very popular during prohibition. What were the men who chased them down called?

They were revenue officers.

196) How long were the early car license plates good for?

As long as you owned your car.

197) What was Little Orphan Annie's favorite saying?

Leaping Lizards.

198) Long ago when a bed sheet wore thin in the middle, how did the thrifty homemaker lengthen its life?

She cut it in half down the middle and sewed the outside edges together to make it strong in the middle again.

199) Long ago, underwear was not always purchased in the store. It was made from a fabric used in packaging. Where did the material come from?

Feed sacks. Often sugar came in the sacks that were used for underwear.

200) Gypsies were a familiar sight long ago. What might they wear that you would recognize they were Gypsies?

Bright clothes, many bracelets, scarves tied at the back of their heads, necklaces, big hoop earrings.

100 ONE-LINE DISCUSSION STARTERS

DO YOU REMEMBER . . .

* The old toaster that looked like a grater?

* When a little piece of charchol was thrown in the meat to sweeten it?

* The bucket brigade?

* The *Regina* that was a flat type hat and worn on one side of the head?

* The Ziegfield Follies and how every year Ziegfield picked a Ziegfield girl, the cream of the crop, for his follies?

* When Physical Education was called *hygiene?*

* When the Red Cross asked you to save peach pits to make mask filters?

* The childhood book *Bears of Blue River?*

* When the yellow daisy or daffodil was the sign that you were for women's sufferage?

* Before city garbage pickup when folks used to dump their garbage in the river?

* When most towns had a city band?

* *Seraco Specific*, a product to break the tobacco habit and how it sold for 29 cents in 1909?

* When eggs were seven cents a dozen and butter was eleven cents a pound?

* In 1909 when you could buy a nice oak rocker for $2.45?

* The bike made without brakes on which you dragged your feet or jumped off to stop?

* When Indians would walk right into your house without saying anything and you would give them something and they would leave?

* When mail was delivered on motorcycles?

* WPA paintings in post offices?

* Steam heat radiators equipped with warming ovens and how some models provided for charchol to be used when the furnace was turned off?

* When you thought nothing of walking a mile to church due to gasoline shortage?

* Houseboats where people lived on the river?

* When the first *Life* magazine was a humor magazine and how Henry Luce bought the title to be used for his glossy pictorial some time later?

* Henry Ford's saying "History is bunk."?

* Wedding celebration where if you ran out of food you just put on a pot of beans?

* For Saturday night's entertainment going to the court house and parking around it and visiting with everyone else who came?

* The old school bank where kids learned to save money?

* When you went into the woods how you would tie your pants legs shut and put kerosene on it to keep mosquitos from biting?

* When you were tickled to death to be offered a ride in a two-seater surrey?

* When Woodrow Wilson said the automobile was a "rich man's play thing?"

* The little laundry stove?

* When oil was five-cents a gallon?

* When the newspaper was delivered to your house for 25 cents a week?

* When you could get a bucket of beer filled at the tavern for ten cents?

* The shoe shine boy who met trains and also set up shop in the barber shops?

* Artesian wells?

* The old drug store where you didn't need a prescription, where you just told the druggist your problem and he fixed you up?

* Before canning jars, how you just saved any glass lidded jars you could get your hands on?

* Grinding coffee beans at home in the little wooden box with the turn handle on the top and a little drawer at the bottom to catch the ground coffee?

* Seeing a line of drays at the old train stations ready to transport the merchandise brought in by train?

* Moving when the moving company arrived with a big wagon and a team of horses?

* Using quinine as a cold killer?

* Buying pickles in a big wooden barrel at the store?

* The medicine shows?

* Around 1914 how you could buy an egg, two strips of bacon and toast for 15 cents?

* The old plank roads?

* Wooden sidewalks?

* When Main Street was dirt and had to be sprinkled to keep the dust down?

* Remember how telephone poles lined Main Street?

* Remember hitching posts and horse tanks along Main Street?

* When money was tight how you bought an ice cream cone for the children but never one for yourself?

* How a building would be rented in town and wax figures would be brought in for a show?

* When folks had their ears pierced thinking it would help their eyes?

* When everyone drank from a common ladle or tin cup at school?

* Chalk boards hanging by ropes from the classroom ceiling?

* When schools didn't hire married women to teach?

* When you didn't need a license to drive a car?

* When you could get a mechanic anywhere to fix a flat tire for 35 cents?

* When you collected rain water in barrels as it drained from the corners of your roof and boiled it and used it for drinking purposes?

* Remember saving rain water to wash your hair?

* The saying, *the cat's pajamas?*

* In 1927 when you could buy a Fordson tractor and a plow for just $700?

* Plucking the goose nearly bald for his feathers and then turning him loose?

* When with some illnesses, the doctor would have you burn the sick person's clothes to avoid contamination?

* When the razor strap was used to sharpen the straight edge razor?

* When streets were paved with brick?

* Hobble skirts?

* The popular black taffeta skirt of the 30's that rustled when you walked and was worn with a white blouse?

* The Homburg, a hat with a high crown and narrow brim?

* The Panama hat?

* Getting to ride in an open cock-pit plane for $2.00 a ride?

* Remember flying shows and wing-walkers?

* Remember how on the first day of June men switched from regular hats to straw ones and on labor day switched back to winter ones?

* Going to an inn, falling asleep, and waking up to find one or two extra people in your bed?

* Mosquito bar?

* Smearcase cheese?

* When you purchased margarine white and had to add your own yellow coloring?

* Using waterglass to keep eggs all winter?

* The school hack drawn by horses?

* Corn selling for 25 cents a bushel and a bale of hay selling for 75 cents?

* The Reo built by Oldsmobile?

* Vulcanizing or tire patching?

* Pouring blackberry wine over tobacco before chewing it?

* When it snowed how it came through the cracks in your roof and how you woke up in the morning with snow all over your bed covers?

* Cookies being buried in oats to mail safely?

* The daybed?

* Remember how when you rode the interurbans you paid a penny per mile traveled?

* Flag pole sitting?

* The livery stables?

* The first time you saw a car and how people would walk to town to see one?

* In the 1930's when all it took to be happy was a Pinochle deck and a sack of popcorn?

* Floppy mob bathing cap?

* Electric perms?

* *Liberty* magazine in the 20's?

* Al Capone's bullet proof Cadillac with a machine gunner beside the driver escorted by a scout car and followed by a posse?

* Mutt and Jeff and Jiggs bringing up father?

* In the 1920's, working 12-hour days for $1.50?

* Invasion money issued to soldiers when they got to Germany during the war?

* When you took burned out light bulbs to the electric company to be replaced with new ones?

* In the 1930's when banks could borrow from the federal reserve for just 3% interest?

* Orsen Wells *War of the Worlds?*

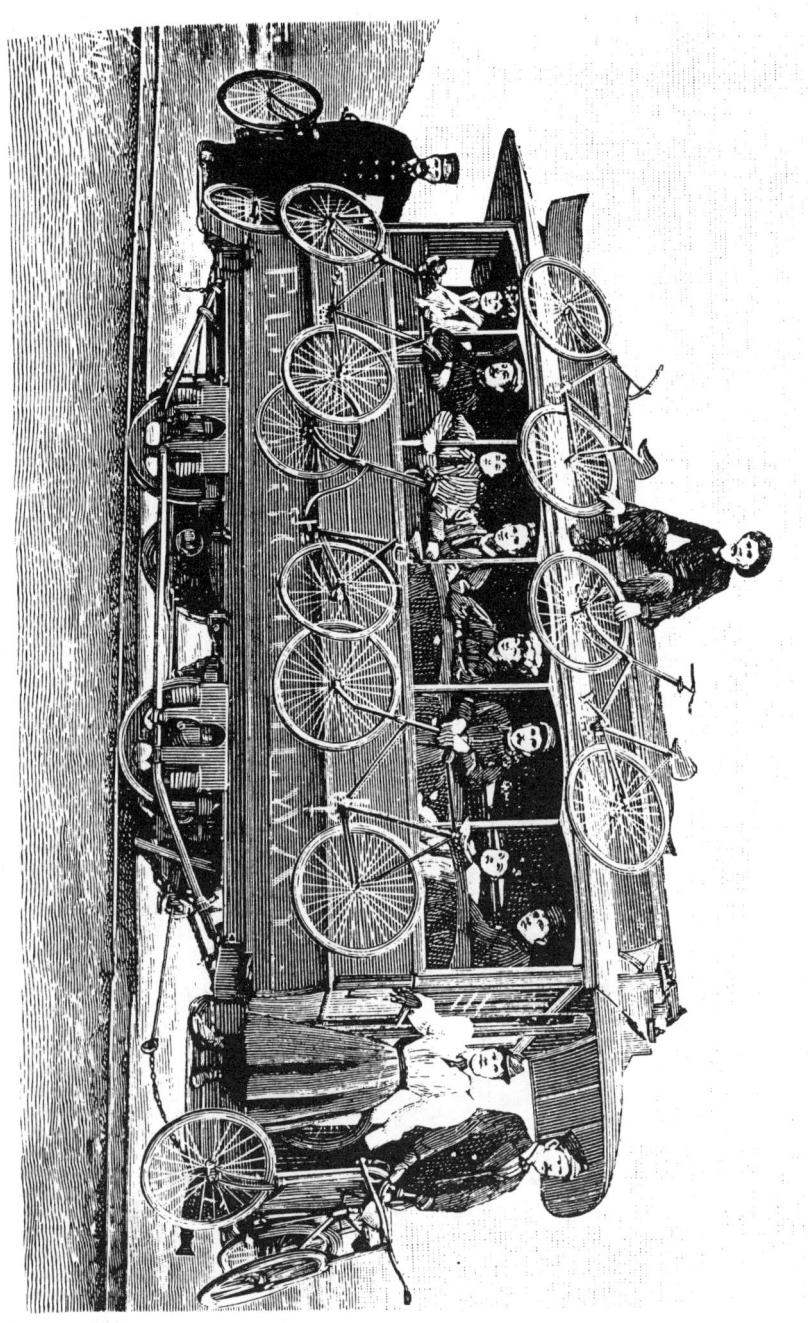

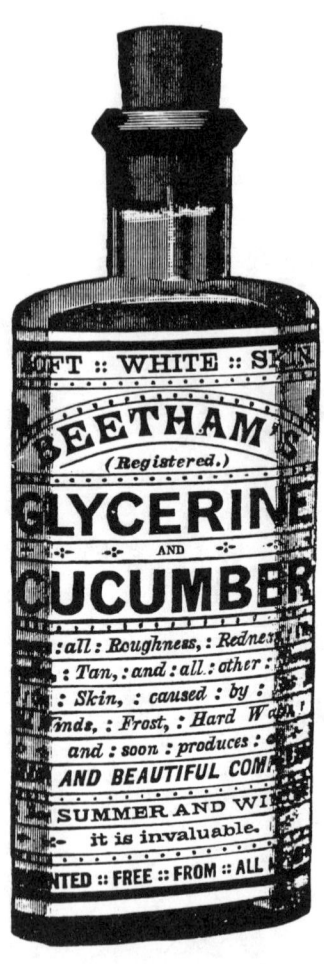

HOME COOKING

Remember the days long ago when no Pop-Tart or hurried bowl of frosted flakes would pass as a self-respecting breakfast? Those were the days when breakfast was a real meal. It might consist first of uncured meat or sausage or bacon left from butchering day. Next there would be a heaping plate of fried potatoes topped with two or three fried eggs, fresh from the hen house. You may remember eating fresh hot biscuits soaked in gravy or spread with sorghum molasses. Or perhaps luscious cornmeal mush started the evening before by stirring cornmeal into boiling water and cooking it till thick. It was then cooled and shaped into a roll and the next morning it was sliced and fried in sizzling lard. You almost begin to lick your lips just thinking about this delicacy served up on a Blue Willow plate dripping with fresh churned butter and hot maple syrup. Another old favorite was buckwheat cakes mixed with yeast the night before and left to raise and be fried at breakfast.

Rolled oats and fried muffins were old standbys. There were homemade jellies, jams and preserves, many made without benefit of Sure-Gel or bottled pectin. They were cooked with sugar for a long while till thick. Raspberries, elderberries, plums and some kinds of apples made good spreads. Spiced tomato preserves, quince marmalade and plum butter were old favorites.

Farmers heading in from the fields stepped just a little faster when they got a whiff of the sweet aroma of apple butter cooking in the big iron pot out in the yard. Bread was baked weekly, usually on Saturdays. When it was rising, cakes and pies would be baked. Sugar cream pies were a real treat.

When someone was sick, milk toast was served. This was a slice of toast on a plate covered with milk and sprinkled with brown or white sugar. Older folks often poured coffee over their toast and sprinkled sugar on it.

Potato soup with drop noodles made a good meal as did canned sausage or head cheese which was a hog's head boiled in water which was then thickened with cornmeal. There was nothing like those dill pickles made in big crocks and covered with grape leaves. Then there was chicken soup, spiced peaches, jam cake and pie crust snacks. These were rolled out pie crust that was spread with butter and sprinkled with cinnamon and sugar and baked. Cinnamon rolls were good as were big sugar cookies. Pineapple upside down cake was a special delicacy but not as good a jelly cake.

With our busy lives today, we're thankful for *McDonald's* and *Pizza King*, but while we're enjoying them, it's fun to let our minds wander back to the good old days and some real good home cooking.

CHILD'S PLAY

Today it's television, electronic toys and computer games. Remember the days when a child was happy with a piece of string--how making *crow's feet* and *Jacob's ladders* would keep him content for hours. Remember playing in the hay mow, swinging on grape vines and diving off a stump into the old creek?

What ever happened to those good old days--days when you made whistles out of river cane and carved instruments that played music and little boats from soft wood? Remember those days when a sling shot made from a fork in a branch and a piece of old inner tube was a prized possession? Remember as children making paw paw whips by peeling bark off a tree? Remember using a wooden spool and a piece of string to make rattle bones which were used to make noise when you drug them across someone's window on Halloween night? Remember those late night games of *hide and seek* and *kick the can?* How about *duck on Davey, Annie Annie over, and shinney on your own side?*

There were paper dolls cut from the Sunday paper, magazines or the *Sears* catalog. There were games of *hopscotch* and roller skating on wooden-wheeled skates. Playing *jacks* was a favorite for girls, and both boys and girls liked the rubber balls attached to wooden paddles with a rubber string. If families could afford them, girls had tricycles and boys had bicycles. In winter ice skates were a favorite, and in summer most kids had a scooter to ride with one foot and push with the other. City kids sometimes had a swimming pool open three days a week for boys to swim and two days for girls. It was considered indecent for them to swim together. And those were the days when some folks even recall making their own balls with which to play from old rags and string.

Remember some of your favorite toys? How about a little

wooden coaster wagon or a special teddy bear with a red wagon to pull him in? How about a rag doll made from quilt blocks and stuffed with sawdust? Remember the toy steam engine that you put water in for steam and also wood alcohol which was lit with a match? Remember how when it got hot enough, it would go? Remember the china head dolls that were often just to look at, not to play with? Then there were the miniature dishes made from real china for very young ladies tea parties. And some girls even received naked dolls, and it was up to them to make the clothes and dress them?

In these hectic days when children become more and more aware of the complexities of life through the use of modern toys, it's nice to remember the days when kids were content with the little things in life--like a piece of string.

***

THE MOVIE SCENE

1930

Remember Maureen O'Sullivan and Johnny Weissmuller in Tarzan?

How about Katharine Hepburn? Remember how she appeared on stage in *The Warrior's Husband* which was a sure hit and how it landed her a chance at film where she began in *A Bill of Divorcement?*

Remember *What Price Hollywood* with Constance Bennett and Lowell Sherman, the first of films showing the inside of Hollywood's great industry of manufacturing, glamour, personality and entertainment?

Remember *The Dark Horse* starring Bette Davis and Warren William?

How about *Love Affair* with Dorothy Mackaill and Humphrey Bogart?

Remember *Westward Passage* with Laurence Olivier and Ann Harding?

Remember *The Bird of Paradise* with Joel McCrea and Dolores Del Rio, the fable of a lovely native girl and a white man?

Remember *Pack Up Your Troubles*, a comedy starring Laurel and Hardy?

Remember *Night After Night*, the gangster film with Mae West and George Raft?

Remember the comedy *Speak Easily* starring Jimmy Durante and Buster Keaton?

How about *Grand Hotel* with Joan Crawford and Lionel Barrymore and Greta Garbo.

Remember the comic strip film *Little Orphan Annie* starring Mitzi Green?

Other Books by the Author

Newsletters Simplified! Don't let the name mislead you. Its 352 pages are packed full of fascinating information for newsletters--YES! But it's ALSO for those who lead activities; for those who like to impress friends with unusual tidbits of information; for those who like history or nostalgia; and for those who enjoy reading and learning. Included are five great chapters on writing, layout and design, article types, proofreading, marketing, and more. **BUT THAT'S JUST THE BEGINNING.** You'll find another 12 chapters of information to include "in" your newsletter. These consist of startling facts, statistics and tidbits, presidential anecdotes and presidential trivia, quotable quotes, helpful hints, facts about historical celebrities (Lindbergh, Earhart, Rockwell, Will Rogers, Shirley Temple, Dionne Quintuplets, Teddy Roosevelt, John Dillinger). You'll also find complete reminiscent articles to print in your newsletter; a rich history of 55 holidays and holy days, funny stories and interesting experiences related by seniors, old-time prices, 15 pages of *Do You Remember?* one liners, comforting scriptures, and 15 full-page historical photographs. ISBN 0-927935-06-6.

Activity Planning at Your Fingertips provides all the activities you'll ever need. Over 600 are presented with complete directions for each. Also featured are three years of pre-planned activity calendars that you are free to copy and use. *Activity Planning at Your Fingertips* is a user-friendly guide created especially for the busy professional who's short on time but desires to be long on activities. The book is divided into ten tabbed sections, and then each section is alphabetized to help you locate any activity in just seconds. There's activity ideas for bedside residents, for low-functioning residents and for more alert and active residents. There's holiday parties, family parties, cooking, crafts, exercise, games, word games, fill-ins, Christmas, men only, outings, clubs, community outreaches, special projects, monthly biggies, and everyday activities. It's a big 208 pages, professionally wiro-bound, ISBN 0-927935-03-01.

other books by Marge Knoth, continued...

The Professional Activity Director is a complete handbook covering most subjects pertinent to activity directors. These include recognizing and developing your professionalism, getting great press coverage, organizing your department, calendar planning made easy, involving your community in your activities, developing and maintaining a workable volunteer program, beating burnout, handling problems common to A.D.'s, planning interesting outings for residents, building an incubator and hatching chicks, planning a district-wide nursing home olympics, word games, a host of new activity ideas, special helps for A.D.'s, and much more. ISBN 0-927935-00-7.

Remembering the Good Old Days, **Lively Reminiscent Group Starters** is designed to let you hold an *old-days* discussion group without any preliminary preparation. Just open to any page, and there you have an *old-days* subject ready to discuss. Numerous questions are provided on each subject which will quickly draw the elderly into discussion. Features 100 nostalgic subjects: old-time beauty secrets, barn dances, immigration, sports, death, toys and games, weddings, dance marathons, the milkman, the iceman, farming, housekeeping, food preservation, famous people, and more. Lots of old-time illustrations and 21 tips for leading a lively reminiscence group. ISBN 927923-02-3

Books may be ordered from:

Valley Press
P.O. Box 5224
Lafayette, IN 47903

About the Author...

Marge Knoth in *Looking Back* discusses one of her favorite subjects--life between 1890 and 1945. She treats you to a nostalgic look back at an era when life was less complicated and people took time to be neighborly. She has been a professional writer since 1974 and spent nine of those writing years as a professional activity director as well. During that time she gained a wealth of first-hand information from the elderly. She is the author of five successful books. *The Professional Activity Director* and *Activity Planning at Your Fingertips* are both national award winners which are being used throughout the U.S. and Canada. They are also used as teaching manuals in colleges and trade schools and by state health care associations. *Newsletters Simplified* is her latest book. *Remembering the Good Old Days* is also about yesteryear. In addition to her books, she has been published in *Family Circle, Christian Science Monitor, Lady's Circle, Women's Circle, True Story, True Love, Indianapolis Woman, Parker's Gazette* and numerous other publications. She writes a monthly column, "A Letter From Marge" for *The Activity Director's Guide*. Marge travels widely and is a regular speaker at activity professional's conventions and workshops. She is a member of the *National Association of Activity Professionals*, the *National Federation of Press Women* and their *Women's Press Club of Indiana* affiliate. She has been active in *Women in Communication* and is a co-founder of *Authors and Friends*. She has been happily married to her best friend, Rick, for almost 34 years and is the mother of four grown children. A very meaningful part of her life is her six beautiful grandchildren: Sarah, Kristin, Matthew, Alec, Collin and Cody.